Dabblers & Divers

A DUCK HUNTER'S BOOK

Ducks Unlimited, Inc.
Memphis, Tennessee
1996

and

Willow Creek Press
Minocqua, Wisconsin
1996

Editor: CHUCK PETRIE
Managing editor: CHRIS DORSEY
Book Design: CECILE BIRCHLER
Photography editor: DIANE JOLIE

Cover Photograph by MARC EPSTEIN
Color Separations and Prepress: WISCONSIN TECHNICOLOR,
Pewaukee, WI

Dabblers & divers : a duck hunter's book.
    p.   cm.
  ISBN 1-57223-068-1 (hardcover : alk. paper)
  1. Waterfowl shooting--Pictorial works.   I. Ducks Unlimited.
SK331.D26 1996
799.2'4841--dc20   96-24436
                                                CIP

ISBN 1-57223-068-1

Published July 1996

Printed in Canada

To the ducks, the wetlands they inhabit,
and to those conservationists who revere and sustain them.

DUCKS UNLIMITED, INC.

The mission of Ducks Unlimited is to fulfill the annual life cycle needs of North American waterfowl by protecting, enhancing, restoring and managing important wetlands and associated uplands. Since its founding in 1937, DU has raised more than $968 million, which has contributed to the conservation of over seven million acres of prime wildlife habitat in all fifty states, each of the Canadian provinces and in key areas of Mexico. In the U.S. alone, DU has helped to conserve over 914,000 acres of waterfowl habitat. Some 600 species of wildlife live and flourish on DU projects, including many threatened or endangered species.

PHOTO CREDITS

FOREWORD

Celebrating the Waterfowler

On rare occasion, a sporting book emerges that takes us back to favorite haunts and rekindles the excitement of opening day. For the wildfowler, that book is *Dabblers & Divers*, a tribute to duck hunting and the exuberance and reverence that envelopes this absorbing pastime. With every turn of the page, you'll sense the allure of a marsh awakening at dawn, feel the chill of a north wind, or chuckle at the antics of a retriever.

Waterfowling is perhaps the most storied of our sporting pursuits, having inspired a rich treasury of insightful prose and memorable lyrics. These pages recount those timeless passages and share the moments of elation, humor, and reflection that make duck hunting the intriguing, captivating sport that it is. Accompanying the text is a selection of stunning photographs, images that capture the drama and beauty of marshland vigils. Through the marriage of words and pictures, *Dabblers & Divers* is the most vivid portrayal of the waterfowler's life ever published.

These colorful vignettes tell the story of the wildfowler. They are treasures of musings and witticisms that paint a portrait of the sportsmen and women who pay homage to the ducks each autumn. Because of their marshland pilgrimages and an abiding reverence for backwaters and sloughs, duck hunters have long worked to preserve these fragile wetland habitats. No group, in fact, has done more to champion conservation efforts than have hunters, the patrons and stewards of our nation's wildlife riches.

This book is also a celebration of waterfowling's heritage, and any hunter whose pulse quickens at the sound of whistling wings will cherish it for years to come. No matter when you open the cover of *Dabblers & Divers*, duck season will be as close as the turn of a page.

MATTHEW B. CONNOLLY
Executive Vice President,
Ducks Unlimited, Inc.

Dabblers & Divers

A D U C K H U N T E R ' S B O O K

*B*eside the sea or away from it, whether by lake, bay, pond, river, or inland marsh, one hides, or remains motionless and waits... Whatever the place, the magic is the same, and for a little while man forgets his mundane duties and enters the primitive world of the hunter, responding to an urge that is as valid as the desire to love a woman or beget a child.

— NELSON BRYANT, *"The Wildfowler's World"*

A hunter should have the best. He owes it to himself, and to the game. He owes it to the dog to let her become what her blood directs her to become: not a player in a stylized game, but a partner, a collaborator, a fellow predator in the fields and thickets, on the trembling, savage ground of the marsh.

— CHARLES FERGUS, A Rough-Shooting Dog

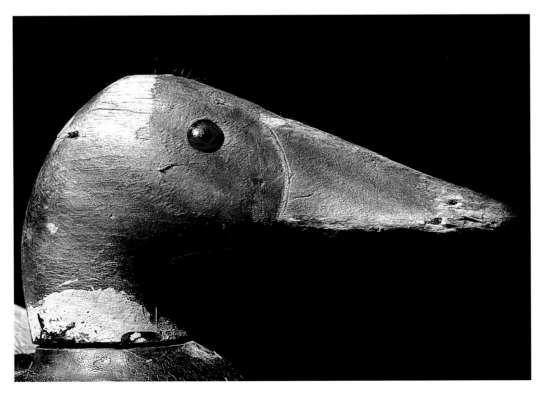

*I*n that chunk of wood or cork that is a decoy lies man's attempt to imitate nature, to fit in with her schemes so perfectly that a beautiful, wise, wild creature will be lured to a hunter. More than any other symbol of waterfowling, the decoy is the essence of its charm and intrigue.
— NORM STRUNG, Misty Mornings and Moonless Nights

A *hunting club is more than a roof over your head and a place to play cards and drink. It is part of a legacy of secret hunting societies that trace back to the Paleolithic, an island of heritage that serves to focus attention on the magic of the spirit of hunting.*
— JAMES A. SWAIN, In Defense of Hunting

I have known many meat eaters to be far
more non-violent than vegetarians.
— MAHATMA GANDHI

On the rare occasion that a person lands himself in the midst of truly wild county, the kind of place that speaks to the soul, it's important to be alone and to listen. Man endlessly creates civilization, but what he truly craves is wilderness. The mere fact that it cannot be built makes it all the more appealing, as its value is in its limitedness.

— CHRIS DORSEY, *"Treasured Islands"*

They'll buck freezing, four-foot waves for a quarter-mile to make a retrieve, and that night by the fire, lie with their favorite stuffed bunny and woof and arf in their sleep. They'll stand between you and a stranger at the door, hackles raised, rumbling a warning only a fool would ignore, and dare danger to enter; two hours later, they'll be yapping at the neighbor kids, trying to worm their way into a game of touch football. If we have to travel away overnight, we know those we love are guarded, safe and protected, by a canine radar installation who will patrol the house, count noses, and sleep lightly against the perils of darkness.

— STEVE SMITH, *Just Labs*

I'll get by with a little help from my friends.
— THE BEATLES, *from the song "Do You Need Anybody"*

*P*rovidence gave me three sons, only about a year and a half apart;
and since it was not possible for me to give them what we usually call
the advantages of wealth, I made up my mind to do my best by them.
I decided primarily to make them sportsmen, for I have a conviction
that to be a sportsman is a mighty long step in the direction of being a
man. I thought also that if a man brings his sons up to be hunters,
they will never grow away from him.

— ARCHIBALD RUTLEDGE, *"Why I Taught My Boys to be Hunters"*

*S*omething hurried by overhead, and I turned to watch. Gee-whil-likens! Three hundred bluebills if there was one, bunched low, ripping the dawn. They slid downhill. The air was still, and I heard the excit-ing "ha-a-a-a-sh" as feathered muscles bit into the wind on the descent.
— GORDON MACQUARRIE, *"Make Mine Bluebills"*

How a hunter can come to see hunting as a spiritual practice and the animals hunted as sacred is a psychology that seems fraught with contradictions, but with an open mind and patience, the validity of these views can be understood and the truth becomes as clear as the sky on a crisp October day.

— JAMES A. SWAN, In Defense of Hunting

The waterfowler who lures birds to decoys is like a painter, working his canvas in the half-light of morning to create an illusion of nature and life. His raw materials are water, marsh, blocks of wood, and a sense of proportion.

— NORMAN STRUNG, Misty Mornings and Moonless Nights

I shifted my stance, parted the brush in front of me, braced myself in good shooting position, got set.

They were swinging in now, a matter of seconds and they would be in range. Perennials, storms windows, fertilizer and shrubbery, what piddling, mediocre stuff. This was worth dying for.

— SIGURD OLSON, *"A Shift In the Wind"*

*T*here is much to be said in behalf of the solitary way of fishing and hunting. It lets people get acquainted with themselves. Do not feel sorry for the man on his own.

— GORDON MACQUARRIE, *"Nothing To Do For Three Weeks"*

*T*here is something about being alone, particularly in wild places, that is very difficult to describe. Do not attempt it if you are subject to nostalgia, for when night comes even the leaves of the trees whisper to you. They bring messages from friends far away, and you feel that you must answer them, and you cannot, except in spirit.

— BERT CLAFLIN, *"Dusky Ducks In the Wilderness"*

What would the world be, once bereft
Of wet and of wildness?
Let them be left,
O let them be left, wildness and wet;
Long live the weeds and the
wilderness yet.

— GERARD MANLEY HOPKINS

An old gun will carry the toothmarks of long-dead craftsmen, the scars of hard hunts completed before you were born, the smooth patina left by the hand of an earlier generation. When today's hunters use such guns, they carry an extra magic that I cannot define, but must acknowledge. And if you acquire a new gun, you are starting a chain that may extend into the future as long as hunters welcome the fall.

— STEPHEN BODIO, Good Guns Again

*H*unting is one of the last genuine, personal adventures of modern man. Just as game animals are the truest indicators of quality natural environment, so hunting is the truest indicator of quality natural freedom.

— JOHN MADSON, Out Home

*T*he pintail is the wariest of all the ducks we shoot along the Texas coast with the possible exception of the widgeon. He is suspicious of everything, even of the other sprigs flying with him, as is demonstrated by the fact that he insists on flying in formation so he can see that every other pintail in the flock is accounted for.

— HART STILLWELL, *"Redhead Ridge"*

While I confess that I view jump-shooting ducks a little like I do prostitution--something more to be pitied than censored--this aspect of waterfowling does have its devotees.
— Norman Strung, Misty Mornings and Moonless Nights

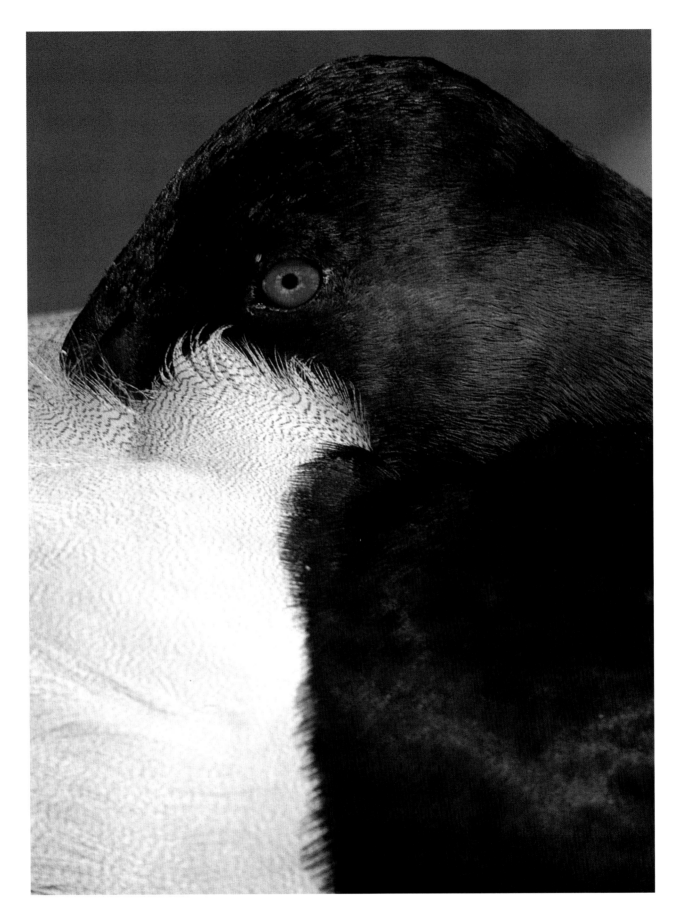

Aside from its reputation as a table delicacy, there is something regal and outstanding about the canvasback. All of its actions are full of character. The big, white body that seems to sit so high on the water, surmounted by the slender-shaped head on the long, thick neck, forms a striking picture. But when the flock is in full flight the big birds are seen at their best. There is such power expressed in the speed and directness of their driving flight, usually made in line formation, that it seems to stamp the "can" as a superduck wherever he is found.

— ALLAN BROOKS, National Geographic *magazine, October, 1934*

Duck hunters are found nearly everywhere--on small creeks, in great marshes, gun shops, pot holes, retriever trials, swamps, slipping out of back doors, telling lies during working hours at the office, and in the pin oaks. Mothers are patient with them, young girls are suspicious of them, wives give up on them, brothers and sisters think they are peculiar, the boss envies them, and Artemis protects them. A duck hunter is Truth with freezing feet, Beauty in long flannels, Wisdom during a gale, and the Hope of the future with Nature as his God.

— CHARLES DICKEY,
"What Is a Duck Hunter"

I am glad to live, glad in my own cunning and strength, glad that I am a doer of things, a doer of things for myself. Of what other reason to live than that? Why should I live if I delight not in myself and the things I do? And it is because I delight and am glad that I go forth to hunt and fish, and it is because I go forth to hunt and fish that I grow cunning and strong. The man who stays in the lodge by the fire grows not cunning and strong. He is not made happy in the eating of my kill, nor is living to him a delight. He does not live.

— JACK LONDON, *"In the Forests of the North"*

It is partly this heritage, I think, that motivates waterfowlers. Keeping a rig in good repair, maintaining a duckboat, arising at three in the morning, and subjecting yourself to the worst weather nature can dish out is hard work--certainly more work than today's low limits would justify, if killing a duck were at the center of a waterfowler's universe.

— NORMAN STRUNG, Misty Mornings and Moonless Nights

Thus we see that the lot of the duck hunter is not a happy one. He is the child of frustration, the collector of mishap, the victim of misfortune. He suffers from cold and wet and lack of sleep. He is punished more often than rewarded. Yet he continues. Why? Because one great day--and great days do come, days when the ducks are willing and the gun swings true--repays him manyfold for all the others.

— Ted Trueblood, "This Mania Called Duck Hunting"

*T*here's duck hunting, and then there's duck hunting in the timber. Each morning casts another spell, for there's nothing like flooded timber. Nothing at all.

— CHRIS DORSEY, *"Timber Legends"*

*I*n both diver and dabbler shooting, this is the moment of truth. Never believe the man who says he can tell what the ducks are going to do before they do it. Most days, the ducks don't even know until it happens. Do you wait and hope they come in? Do you take them on the first pass? Do you wait for two passes?

— STEVE SMITH, Hunting Ducks and Geese

Wise is the wild duck winging straight to the river of summer!
From the cold arctic sea, coming, like his fathers for centuries,
to seek the sweet, salt pastures of the far Chesapeake...

— GEORGE ALFRED TOWNSEND

_To_ those of us who know it well, wildfowling holds some special magic, something available only from the world of water and wind, of mud stiff with cold, of black dogs and long guns. It's a world well worth the caring for. If we can no longer participate in the same way that our grandfathers did, we still can capture the feeling, and in the feeling lies the key.

— MICHAEL MCINTOSH, _"Gunning the Grand Passage"_

We need the tonic of wildness--to wade sometimes in marshes where the bittern and the meadow-hen lurk, and hear the booming of the snipe; to smell the whispering sedge where only some wilder and more solitary fowl builds her nest, and the mink crawls with its belly close to the ground.

— HENRY DAVID THOREAU, Walden

"I suppose," he said, "that when a man quits liking this it's time to bury him."
— GORDON MACQUARRIE,
"Pothole Guys, Friz Out"

Shooting from a layout boat is a lot like trying to hit the rabbits at the carnival shooting gallery--while you're riding the ferris wheel. The layout boat is stable but subject to the whims of the tides and the wind.

— STEVE SMITH, Hunting Ducks and Geese

It is astonishing how much room there is in the air around a duck!
— GEORGE BIRD GRINNELL

*A*nd when everything clicks, it is as if the shotgun were a set of talons or jaws or a beak, a potent extension of the body—one points with the left hand, out in front, gripping the barrels, the shot is loosed, it reaches out from the brain and soul, through wood and metal, through thin air, to intercept the wild fleeting form.

— CHARLES FERGUS, A Rough-Shooting Dog

*T*hey'll skim across the outer edge of your decoy spread and gun range, very nearly tolling on each pass, then stop short, feathering the air, to gain elevation for yet another pass. If you'll blow a few low tones just as they start to set their wings, the invitation is often sufficient to get them to drop right on in. That particular success is one of the sweetest in duck hunting: you feel like you can talk to the animals.

— NORMAN STRUNG, Misty Mornings and Moonless Nights

The rabbit hound believes in his nose and the chase.
The pointing dog believes in his nose and the gun.
The retriever believes in his handler.

— RICHARD WALTERS, The Labrador Retriever

The decoys are set. The gunners are in the blind. The nether cusp of the moon rests upon the horizon to the west. A saffron, pinkish light suffuses the eastern sky and dims the moon. It is a moment of sheer breathless beauty.

— JOHN G. MacKENTY, Duck Hunting

To begin, place the end of the call firmly in your right hand between the thumb and first finger. Place the other end of the call between your lips in front of your teeth, blowing air while saying the word "HOOT.""

— From instruction sheet accompanying
Yentzen Sure-Shot duck call

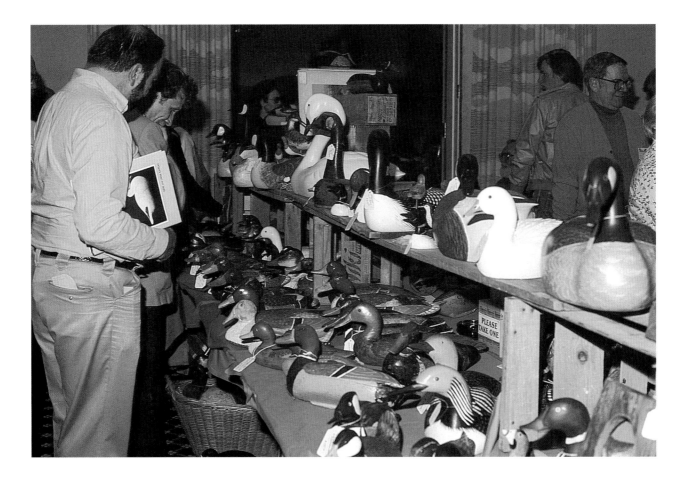

*A*nd so we troop to auction houses to bid on antique decoys of
questionable intrinsic worth, but incalculable symbolic value.
We haunt used-goods stores, searching for duck-hunting
paraphernalia and hang it beside the mantelpiece like an amulet.
— TERRY WIELAND, *"The Other Side of Sport"*

We buy paintings of ducks, and carvings of ducks, and place them about the house--icons that remind us not of hunting we have done or would like to do, but as a link with the past of our fathers.
— TERRY WIELAND, *"The Other Side of Sport"*

*P*erhaps chief to me among the collateral reasons [we hunt ducks]
is the complete opportunity to be one with nature at the time of its
most charming and delightful mood--dawn.
— JOHN G. MACKENTY, Duck Hunting

Have you sat thus on a snowy day and squinted through the white curtain at those mail-carrying bluebills? Have you seen these birds of passage drop from nowhere? All sails set, and come to rest with a swi-i-ish right among the decoys? Birds of passage indeed, but regal birds.

— GORDON MACQUARRIE,
More Stories of the Old Duck Hunters

A band of bluebills came slashing towards me. How fine and brave they are, flying in their tight little formations!

— GORDON MACQUARRIE,
"Nothing To Do For Three Weeks"

*T*he problem today is that you seldom have enough space to properly call ducks into your decoys. You may be a caller of championship caliber, but all the caterwauling around you will nullify your most artistic efforts. You can work on birds for ten minutes and just when they decide to drop in, the guy in the next blind will choose that moment to ground-swat a mudhen and you can watch your birds claw for altitude.

— BOB HINMAN, *The Duck Hunter's Handbook*

*T*he Indians of the Frazer valley tell a story of two men in one of their tribes who had a dispute as to how the whistler made the noise, one claiming it was produced by the wings, the other that it was vocal or made through the nostrils. Others joined in the controversy, which resulted in a majority of the warriors being killed without settling the question.

— DWIGHT W. HUNTINGTON, Our Feathered Game

The retrieved goldeneye was a drake. As I inspected that first drake I felt that somewhere in the northern fastness where he dwells there must be a duck valet who lacquers his short bill, shines his yellow shoes, grooms the snowy, immaculate breast, and as a final touch, affixes the round white boutonniere just below either eye.

— GORDON MACQUARRIE,
More Stories of the Old Duck Hunters

Over the years I have learned that if you accept the weather, its warmth and its wrath, it has a way of invigorating the spirit and satisfying the soul. Sometimes the wind, the rain, the sleet, and the snow are a duck hunter's only reward--each sunrise an adventure, each sunset a covenant of a more abundant tomorrow.

— RICHARD S. GROZIK, *"Distant Wings"*

70

The labrador is the king of retrievers. . .He is intelligent but not cunning; he's lovable but not soft. The Labrador retriever is loyal but not a one-man dog. He's gentle but not a dog to be backed against the wall. He's a romping fun fellow but won his crown as an honest worker.

— RICHARD WALTERS, The Labrador Retriever,

*T*he true devotee of the wind-swept autumn waters hunts many other things besides ducks. He hunts the unfolding secrets of the dawn and the message of the wind. He hunts the curling waves and the tossing tops of suppliant trees. He hunts the poignant loneliness of a tender, departing season and the boisterous advent of one more rigorous. All these he hunts and, old or young, he finds them as they were before--primordial, healing and soothing to mankind in his whirling world of complexities.

— GORDON MACQUARRIE, *"A Pothole Rendezvous"*

*A*nd when you put decoys, days, marshes, and blinds together
so well that birds decoy into your lap, you know you've done
something right, and all the cussing, work, waiting, and past
frustration pale in the reflection of that glorious day.
  — NORMAN STRUNG, Misty Mornings and Moonless Nights

*F*or some, hunting is a pleasant pastime; a chance to get out into the woods, enjoy nature, and maybe shoot something. For those who catch "hunting fever," however, hunting becomes a passion. It takes over garages, guides people to paint boats a dull dead-grass color, moves people to purchase expensive wardrobes that often are worn just a few days of the year, and inspires investment in expensive guns, dogs, decoys, calls, and other equipment.

— JAMES A. SWAN, In Defense of Hunting

*W*hether they fly into our imaginations or float into our thoughts, ducks forever inspire memories of favorite places and special moments.

— CHRIS DORSEY, *"Dabbling With Portraits"*

...pick your gunning companion with the same care and forethought you would employ in selecting a business partner, except that in the testing, I suggest the employment of a finer mesh screen and a stronger acid.

— JOHN G. MACKENTY, Duck Hunting

*B*etween a boy's first single barrel and a wistful old man, we find an amazing creature called a duck hunter. They are found in patched sweaters and cashmere, but all
of them have the same idea: To enjoy every second of every minute of every hunting
trip--and to protest violently at the slowness of the approaching shooting hour and to
give up reluctantly when the sun sets and the hunting ends for the day.

— CHARLES DICKEY, *"What Is a Duck Hunter"*

As to the mysticism, it was in the awe I felt for the ducks and geese, the journeys they took, the hazards they faced, the sheer beauty of them. I'd find myself reduced, as a presence in the universe, in the same way one does when looking at stars, and when a duck fell it had the magic of a falling star. I liked that. I liked hunting alone sometimes, so that I could intensify it with silence and with solitude.

— VANCE BOURJAILY, *A Prefatory Note,*
Early AmericanWaterfowling: 1770's-1930

You get too fond of a dog. Not until after his death do you realize how much he meant to you. I sometimes wonder if the pleasure in owning a good dog is worth the misery caused by his death.

— J.A. HUNTER, *Hunter*

*S*hould you have the satisfaction of seeing him double up, throw his head on his back, and drop like a chunk of lead, his dead body carried by the inertia of his now still wings, following the same angle he mapped out when alive, you can illuminate your blind with your sweetest smile, pat your dog fondly, and mark my word, if the dog is an old duck retriever, you will plainly see in his honest eyes an expressive feeling, showing he appreciates the shot. Don't try this shot too often, lest you fall from grace in the dog's estimation.

—WILLIAM BRUCE LEFFINGWELL, Wild Fowl Shooting

From an expanse of cypress, gum, and gigantic oaks slightly
water-covered and chock full of mast sprang acres of ducks . . .
Hundreds of bewildered birds swept past, sunlight glinting from
plumage—a sight for the Red Gods.

— Nash Buckingham, Bloodlines

A lone mallard swerves into the picture. The drake's hissed greeting to silent, scattered forms; sunlight glinting from a green velvet head. Faith in Nature poised for its rendezvous with fate.

— NASH BUCKINGHAM, *"What Rarer Day"*

If I must choose among the sports that draw me into the open, it will be duck hunting. No other sport with rod or gun holds so much of mystery and drama. The game comes out of the sky."
— Gordon MacQuarrie, *"The Bluebills Died at Dawn"*

A hunter should never let himself be deluded by pride or false
sense of dominance. It is not through our power that we take life
in nature; it is through the power of nature that life is given to us.

— RICHARD NELSON, *"The Gifts"*

To follow the sport in all its ranges calls for a willingness to accept cheerfully indifferent food and accommodations as well as the constant hazard and exposure. With strength and health these are held lightly and there are no limits to the sporting thrills of those who love the whir of wings as day breaks over the waters or the mists drive across the marshes.

— DR. WILLIAM BRUETTE,
American Duck, Goose, and Brant Shooting

*W*hoever said you can't buy hapiness forgot little puppies.

— GENE HILL

*W*aterfowling is about horizons: scanning them and dreaming them.
— CHRIS DORSEY, *"Let the Season Begin"*

If you properly respect what you are after, and shoot it cleanly and on the animal's terrain, if you imprison in your mind all the wonder of the day from sky to smell to breeze to flowers--then you have not merely killed an animal. You have lent immortality to a beast you have killed because you loved him and wanted him forever so that you could always capture the day.

— ROBERT RUARK, The Old Man and the Boy

*I*f the sentimentalists were right, hunting would develop in men a cruelty of character. But I have found that it inculcates patience, demands discipline and iron nerve, and develops a serenity of spirit that makes for long life and long love of life. And it is my fixed conviction that if a parent can give his children a passionate and wholesome devotion to the outdoors, the fact that he cannot leave each of them a fortune does not really matter so much. They will always enjoy life in its nobler aspects without money and without price. They will worship the Creator in his mighty works. And because they know and love the natural world, they will always feel at home in the wild, sweet habitations of the Ancient Mother.

— ARCHIBALD RUTLEDGE, *"Why I Taught My Boys to be Hunters"*

*T*he companionship, the joint and co-operative effort of two or three men stalking a pothole or huddled in a blind or rowing a stubborn boat among the ice cakes after a cripple, seems to engender a relationship that the conflicts and vicissitudes of everyday life cannot impair.

— JOHN G. MACKENTY, *Duck Hunting*

*I*t is hard, earnest, downright work. It requires a man who not only can rough it, but who loves to rough it, for its own sake--who can endure cold, wet, fatigue, and the weariness of long waiting, not only with patience but with pleasure, and at last feel himself well rewarded if he make a good bag, and not altogether unrewarded, if he make a bad one. If he cannot bring himself to this, he would far better stay at home by his cozy fireside, and pretty wife or pleasant friend; and if he be past forty-five years old, I do not know but he were wiser to do so, whether or no.

— FRANK FORESTER, Manual for Young Sportsmen

*E*ach year it is the same. In vain we lecture ourselves with the same old phrases, "It doesn't make sense," "At our age we ought--" etc., etc. And then my hand goes out in the darkness and wraps the cold metal of a flashlight. 3:30 A.M. A gust of chill damp air comes in the window. A few scattered drops of rain splash against the glass. Rough weather ahead. Duck weather. I am on my feet. The light is lit--the marsh. There is no other choice.

— PHILLIP H. BABCOCK, *"New Brunswick"*

*A*ny serious waterfowling is bound to involve its share of rain.
— NORMAN STRUNG, Misty Mornings and Moonless Nights

*To most New England waterfowlers, the black duck is everything.
Whether huddled against the stinging rain out on the edge of a salt
marsh, or crouched down among bare, black, hardwood branches
beside some inland beaver pond, give a grizzled, old Yankee gunner
a grey November day and a brace of black ducks wheeling down out
of the wind-tattered clouds, and his soul will know no hunger.*

— NELSON BRYANT, *"Beyond the Limit"*

Huntsman rest! Thy chase is done.
— Sir Walter Scott

It has always seemed to me that any man is a better man for being a hunter. This sport confers a certain constant alertness, and develops a certain ruggedness of character that, in these days of too much civilization, is refreshing; moreover, it allies us to the pioneer past. In a deep sense, this great land of ours was won for us by hunters.

— ARCHIBALD RUTLEDGE, *"Why I Taught My Boys to be Hunters"*

*T*he next few seconds held the reason why grown men sit in cold, wet, windy blinds on forsaken swampy points hour after hour, neglecting their families and their business affairs, and getting chilblains, to take a few pounds of meat they could purchase with no hardship at all from almost any farmer.

— RUSSELL ANNABEL, *"Skyful of Bright Wings"*

I have always had a soft spot in my heart for marshes. They challenge me to come and look. Their capacity for mothering wildlife is far greater than the drier uplands, no matter how beautiful they may be. It seems to me that no man is closer to the beginning of things and the eternal motherhood of the outdoors than when he is familiar with a marsh.

—GORDON MACQUARRIE,
"Shallow Bay Comes Back"

*T*he outdoors holds many things of keen delight. A deer flashing across a burn, a squirrel corkscrewing up a tree trunk, a sharptail throbbing up from the stubble--all these have their place in my scheme of things. But the magic visitation of ducks from the sky to a set of bobbing blocks holds more of beauty and heart-pounding thrill than I have ever experienced afield with rod or gun. Not even the sure, hard pluck of a hard-to-fool brown trout, or the lurching smash of a river smallmouth has stirred me as has the circling caution of ducks coming to decoys.

— GORDON MACQUARRIE,
More Stories of the Old Duck Hunters

The predominant thing about this marsh is its stench. I don't want to give the impression that the mud smelt evil. Far from it. Sometimes I can succeed in conjuring up that smell from memory. When I do, I experience almost total recall, remembering how a bunch of widgeon flew, the texture of a particular mussel scar, the way a certain red dawn broke.

— COLIN WILLCOCK, *"And Keep Your Powder Dry"*

This, in part, is why he has come here. This, and the difficult beauty of patience in a cold wind, of enticing ducks and geese that have seen decoys before and survived other calls: this, and the smooth gun swing, the report, the plummeting bird, the eagerness of the big black Labrador retriever. It is atavism, no doubt, but also the craftsman's pride and the naturalist's curiosity.

— ROBERT ELMAN, The Atlantic Flyway

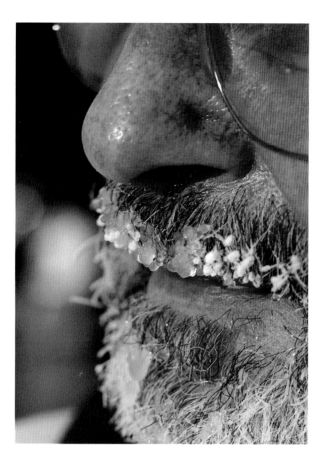

As we huddled, with sleet blasting the skin off our faces and our feet too numb for feeling, he explained to me, through frost-chapped lips, that this nation was nurtured in the Puritan ethic, one tenet of which holds that anything pleasant or enjoyable must, per se, be wicked or sinful, and that wickedness must sooner or later be explained in pain and suffering. Duck hunting, he declared, provides expiation, with the degree of suffering in direct relation to the quality of the sport--since ducks fly best when the weather's worst. I'm not enough of a psychologist to know how valid the doctor's theory is, but I recall that, as I sat there in the blind with my teeth chattering and my hands so chilled I could barely hold a gun, it made a lot of sense.

— ED ZERN, "Wings and Water, Guns and Dogs"

Some teal came in and squished down in the decoys, and I led one a mile and he dropped like a rock. I led another the same mile, and he went on to Mexico.

— ROBERT RUARK,
"A Duck Looks Different To Another Duck"

A flock of forty or fifty blue-winged teal swept over the decoys with all the roar and swishing of air that such a happening can create. The birds were in and gone before either boy knew what it was all about. Then one boy dropped to the ground and hissed to the other: "Git down!"

"What do you want to get down now for?" asked the slower-witted of the two.

"Hell," said the first boy, "the world's round, ain't it? They'll pass us again in a minute."

— RAY P. HOLLAND, *"Waterfowl Speeds"*

*H*unting may lead people to have peak experiences. All the positive elements are there, from spectacular environmental settings to intense emotional excitement, to encounters with the deepest issues of life and death. Many hunters I know feel that ultimately hunting is their religion, but often they do not admit this because of criticism from those who do not understand the hunter's soul.

— JAMES A. SWAN, In Defense of Hunting

A soft breeze again stirs the incredible stillness of the marsh. You smile, suspecting it will blow the rest of the day, and watch as it sets the stool to motion, swinging on their lines. It is so like a flock of real birds that you do a double take, just to make sure a black didn't sneak into the rig when you weren't looking.

Not to shoot--it's still before gunning hours. But a bird coming in while you were still in the rig would be the finishing touch, and a good omen.

You go back to the blind to admire your creation over a cup of coffee; a few puffs on a smoke, and the cold muzzle of your Lab nudging your hand. The dawn explodes in rainbow hues. It's the prettiest time of all; those few introspective moments before the gun.
— NORMAN STRUNG, Misty Mornings and Moonless Nights

*L*ike a dog, he hunts in dreams.
— ALFRED, Lord Tennyson

Hunting is a path, a muddy, brushy, dank, and spoor-written path along which the seeker, if his spirit be right, can truly feel the earth. If he is fortunate, he travels with a true dog and a true friend.

— Charles Fergus, A Rough-Shooting Dog

Admittedly, there are no hard-and-fast rules about what draws or flares waterfowl around decoys--just an interminable bunch of variables that it's up to you to assess. But that's what's so damned intriguing and absorbing about the sport: if you're really waterfowling, you've got not time for the mundane cares of bills, work, wives, or lovers.

— NORMAN STRUNG, Misty Mornings and Moonless Nights

Trying to hit a downwind can is extremely challenging and difficult; doing so is a noteworthy feat.

— STEVE SMITH, Hunting Ducks and Geese

*T*he mallards that came to feed flew high in the air, wheeling round in gradually lowering circles when they had reached the spot where they intended to light. In shooting in the grainfields there is usually plenty of time to aim, a snap shot being from the nature of the sport exceptional. Care must be taken to lie quiet until the ducks are near enough; shots are most often lost through shooting too soon. Heavy guns with heavy loads are necessary, for the ducks are generally killed at long range; and both from this circumstance as well as from the rapidity of their flight, it is imperative to hold well ahead of the bird fired at.

— THEODORE ROOSEVELT, Big Game Hunting

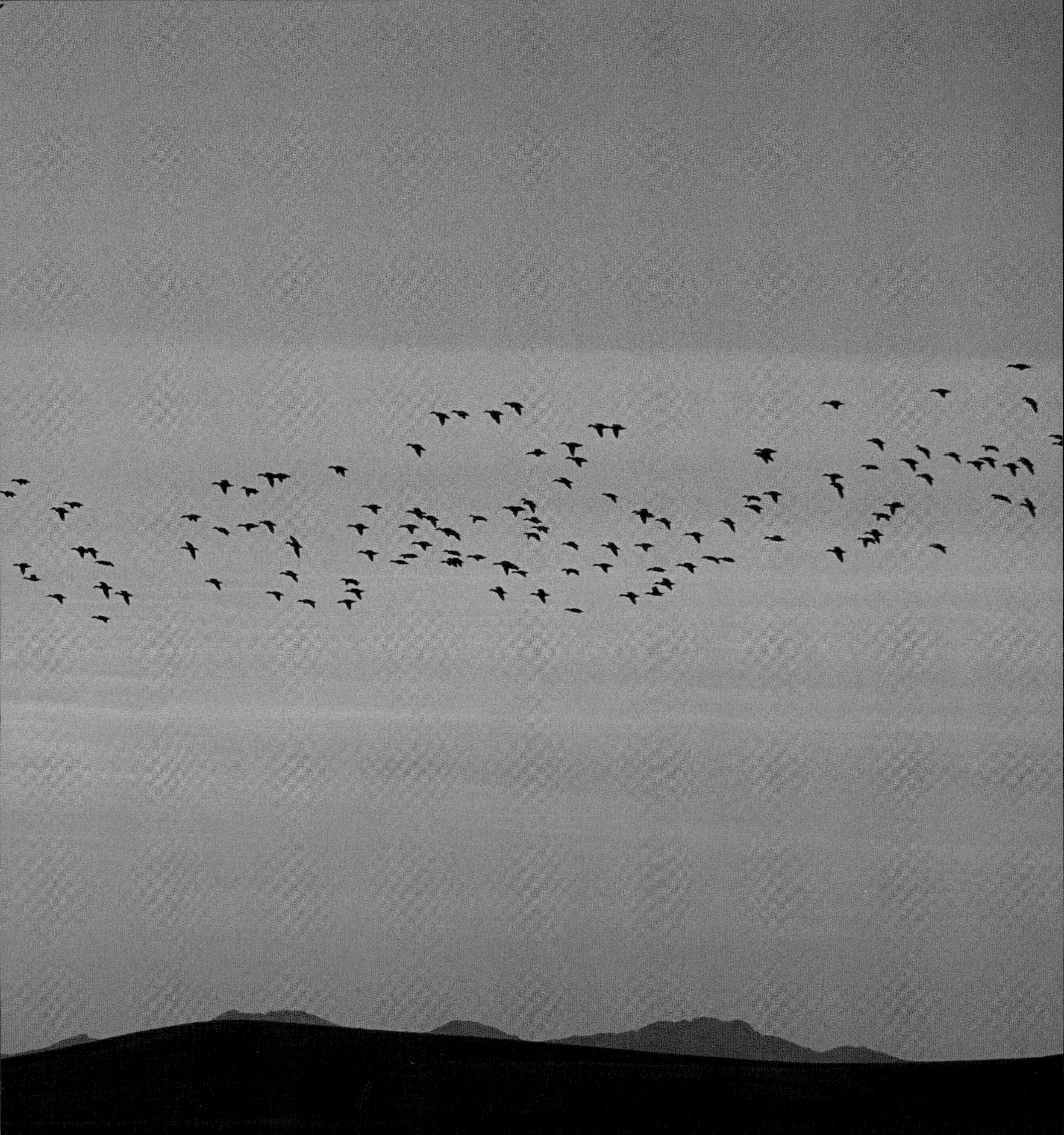

What is religious about hunting is that it leads us to remember and accept the violent nature of our condition, that every animal that eats will in turn one day be eaten. The hunt keeps us honest.

— DUDLEY YOUNG, The Origins of the Sacred

There is also quiet pride that can be savored in memory. Pride in the stamina sometimes required for the enjoyment--genuine, wondering, thanksgiving enjoyment--of the worst weather nature can concoct, the steadfastly nasty kind that is often the best wildfowling weather.

— ROBERT ELMAN, The Atlantic Flyway

*T*he hunter is not a breed apart, nor the wildfowler a distant species: but hunting is a way of life, and my own would have been infinitely poorer without it.

— BOB HINMAN, The Duck Hunter's Handbook

*T*he looking is far more important than the killing when you're hunting with decoys, and a bird tolling directly to you is one of the most beautiful sights in the out-of-doors.

— NORMAN STRUNG, *"Setting Decoys"*

*T*oday Sedam Point is a mere triangle of sand, barely big enough for two blinds, but the hopeful hunters still come. They're no longer baymen, but schoolteachers, students, insurance brokers, and laborers. They come when they can--before work, after school, on their days off--and set their rigs off the point to stare seaward and watch for black duck, broadbill, and an occasional mallard. They don't know the total intimacy that comes with life rooted in an estuary, but still they all share that quality I found so distinctive many years ago: a deep and abiding respect for, and fascination with, waterfowl. They know the delight of three wobbling teal appearing out of nowhere on a misty morning. They are awed by the sounds of a flock of geese passing overhead on a moonless night. They sense the mystery and romance of waterfowl as they follow the sun and fly with the wind to some unknown destiny.

— NORMAN STRUNG, Misty Mornings and Moonless Nights

I do not kill with my gun; he who kills with his gun has forgotten the face of his father. I kill with my heart.

— STEPHEN KING, The Wastelands

Another handy gadget to have is a pair of binoculars. I started carrying some with me a couple of years ago, and they have remarkable uses. You can see how many decoys the other guy has out, sneer at his spread and lack of imagination, and laugh at his choice of shotguns. You can also watch him pick up early with his limit.

— STEVE SMITH, Hunting Ducks and Geese

Ducks fly eternal in the daydreams of sleepy retrievers.
Rest now, good friend, for I'll need you soon.

— CHRIS DORSEY, *"Working Like A Dog"*

The fowler's world of remote and windswept estuaries where geese and duck feed, where waders bustle and fill the air with their plaintive music, is one which has inspired artists and writers for centuries. The wildlfowler is a lucky man and he knows it.
                                    — DAVID S. P. CANT, Modern Wildfowling

Hunters these days ultimately hunt memories as much as meat to put on the table. Memories feed dreams, and hunters must have dreams to keep them motivated. When you lose your dreams, you lose your mind.

— JAMES A. SWAN, In Defense of Hunting

When the wildfowler quits his blind for the season, days have begun to lengthen and some of the birds in southern marshes are growing restless, already yearning for the north. The hunter, watching a little wedge of ducks melt into the horizon, wishes them farewell. He visualizes their arrival at the nesting grounds and thinks about life cycles, sowing and harvesting, eternal renewal, the complex simplicity of his planet. A season's end, he observes with equanimity, is also a season's beginning.

— ROBERT ELMAN, The Atlantic Flyway